by Kate Mason

Troll

Printed in U.S.A.

ISBN 0-8167-3548-4

10 9 8

Contents

Bracelets

Introduction

The best thing about *All-New Friendship Bracelets* is that every bracelet is designed by you. Start by selecting a pattern in this book. Then choose the colors you want and follow the pattern, adding new stitches whenever you feel like it. It's so much fun exchanging these bracelets because each one is one-of-a-kind.

If you've made friendship bracelets before, you'll flip over these new stitches. If you're a rookie, start with one of the easier bracelets in the front of the book like the *Hot Twist* or the *Tiger Tail*. Just follow the instructions and get ready to surprise yourself. These bracelets are a lot easier to make than they look. But that will be *your* secret. Before you know it, you'll be making awesome bracelets like *Speed Racer* or the *Barracuda*. Then you can start combining stitches or you can create your own crazy stitches!

Once you start, you'll be hooked. *All-New Friendship Bracelets* makes having fun as simple as tying a knot!

Once A Bracelet, Always A Bracelet?

Besides wearing friendship bracelets, there are all sorts of other creative things you can do with them. They make awesome bows for gifts instead of ribbon. What about using one as a colorful bookmark? Or even a choker?

You can make great borders for picture frames, pull chains for fans or lights, or decorate handles on lunch boxes. How about rolling a shorter bracelet into a coil and gluing it onto a magnet! It will look great on the refrigerator. And what cat or dog wouldn't want one as an incredibly cool collar? Let your imagination go wild!

What You Will Need

Be sure to have these things handy before you start on your bracelets:

scissors

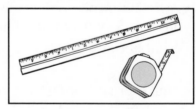

masking tape

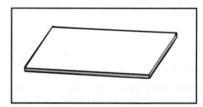

flat surface
like a table top
or a piece of
cardboard

ruler or tape
measure

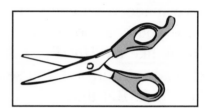

pen

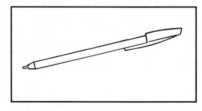

Let's Get Going!

We've included plenty of embroidery string in a rainbow of great colors for you to use. Gather all the materials on page 4 and you're ready to begin!

All the bracelets in this book begin and end with a simple knot. Be sure to leave a 3-inch (7.6-cm) tail of extra string at both ends before tying each knot. You'll use these tails to tie your bracelet closed, as shown below.

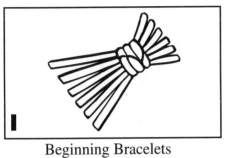

1

Beginning Bracelets

2

Ending Bracelets

One Last Tip

You can label each strand with its corresponding letter and/or number by putting a tiny piece of tape on the end of each strand.

This will help you remember which strand you will use for the next stitch.

Also, taping the ends to a piece of cardboard and placing it on your lap works great. Then you can work on your bracelet wherever you go.

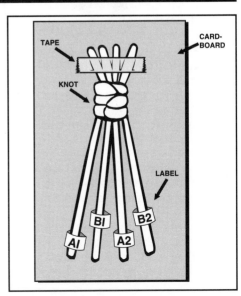

TAPE

CARD-BOARD

KNOT

LABEL

A1 B1 A2 B2

5

HOT TWIST

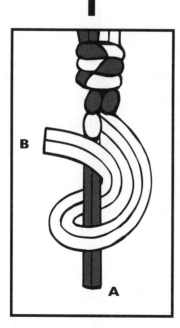

Here's where you'll learn the double-knot stitch that is used to make many of these bracelets. You'll need four 20-inch (51-cm) strands of string. Pick any two colors.

Make a 3-inch (7.6-cm) tail and tie all four strands together. Then tape them to a flat surface. You'll be using both strands of each color as one big strand.

1 Wrap A over and then under B. Hold B tightly and pull A up to the big knot. You have just made the first knot in your double-knot stitch. A is now on the right. Turn the knot so A is on the left side.

2 Use A again to make a second knot around B. Now you have a double knot around B, and A is on the right. Turn the knot so that A is now on the left side.

3 Take B from the right, and wrap it over and then under A. Hold A tightly and pull B all the way up to the previous knot. Repeat so that you have a double knot around A.

4 Keep repeating steps 1-3, so that you alternate double knots from the left and from the right. When your bracelet is long enough, tie the 4 strands together, leave a 3-inch (7.6-cm) tail, and trim the rest off. Tie the bracelet ends together.

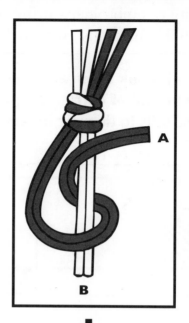

1

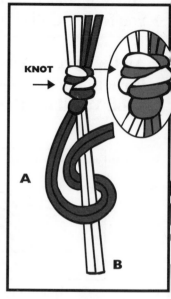

KNOT →

A

A

B

2

B

A

3

A   B

4

TIGER TAIL

You'll need four different colors of string, each 24 inches (61 cm) long. Leave a 3-inch (7.6-cm) tail, tie all four strands together, and tape them to a flat surface. Arrange them in 4 lines (A, B, C, and D).

1 Take the first strand, which is A, and wrap it over and then under B. Pull B tight as you pull A up to the big knot.

2 Repeat Step 1, using A to make a second knot around B. Once you have this double knot, let go of B.

3 Now wrap A over and then under C. Hold C tightly as you pull A up toward the top. Make a second knot around C. Now make a double knot around D.

4 Pick up B and stitch a row of double knots around C, D, and A. The rows of knots should be slanting down toward the right. B will be on the far right.

5 Pick up C and stitch a row of double knots around D, A, and B. Drop C. Pick up D and stitch a row of double knots around A, B, and C. Drop D and start over with A. Make rows of double knots until your bracelet is long enough. Tie the 4 strands together, leave a 3-inch (7.6-cm) tail, and trim the rest off. Tie the bracelet ends together.

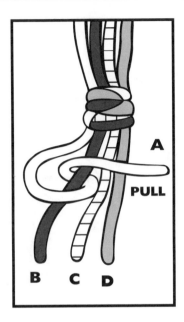

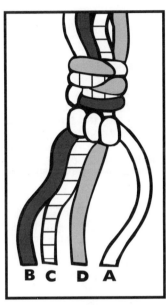

3

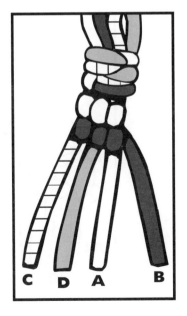

4

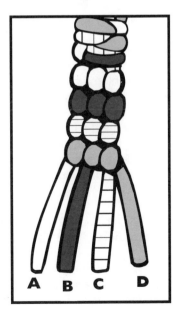

5

7

THE POPSICLE

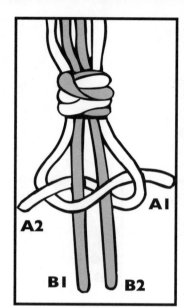

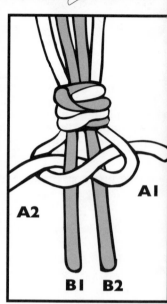

1

2

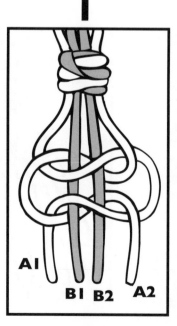

3

4

You'll need two 12-inch (31-cm) strands of one color, and two 30-inch (76-cm) strands of another color. Leave a 3-inch (7.6-cm) tail and tie all four strands together. Tape them to a flat surface. You'll be weaving the two outside strands around the two inside strands.

1 Put the two shorter strands in the middle of the two long strands. The shorter strands will be B1 and B2. The long left strand will be A1 and the long right strand will be A2. Pick up A1 and bring it over B1 and B2, and then under A2. Pick up A2 and bring it under B1 and B2. Then bring it up through the loop you formed with A1.

2 Pull A1 and A2 up to tighten the knot. Keep B1 and B2 very straight in the center. You now have a half-knot.

3 Now bring A1 over B1 and B2, and then under A2. Bring A2 under B1 and B2, and then up through the loop you formed with A1.

4 Pull A1 and A2 up to tighten the knot. Keep B1 and B2 very straight in the center. Now you have a square-knot. Repeat steps 1-4 until your bracelet is long enough. Tie the 4 strands together, leave a 3-inch (7.6-cm) tail, and trim the rest off. Tie the bracelet ends together.

ICE CAPS

Yes, you can believe your eye-balls – the *Ice Caps* starts out like *The Popsicle*. You'll need two 24-inch (61-cm) strands of two colors. Leave a tail and tie all four strands together and tape them to a flat surface. Arrange the strands so that they line up in this order: A1, B1, B2, and A2.

1 Pick up A1 and bring it over B1 and B2, and then under A2. Pick up A2 and bring it under B1 and B2. Then bring it up through the loop you formed with A1. Pull A1 and A2 up to tighten the knot. Keep B1 and B2 very straight in the center. You now have a half-knot.

2 Now bring A1 over B1 and B2, and then under A2. Bring A2 under B1 and B2, and then up through the loop you formed with A1. Pull A1 and A2 up to tighten the knot. Keep B1 and B2 very straight in the center. Now you have a square-knot.

3 Move A1 and A2 into the middle of B1 and B2.

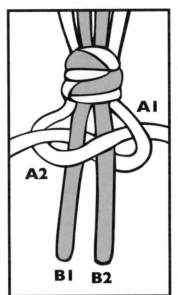

1

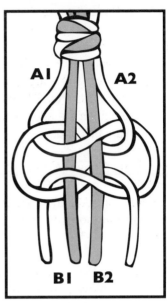

2

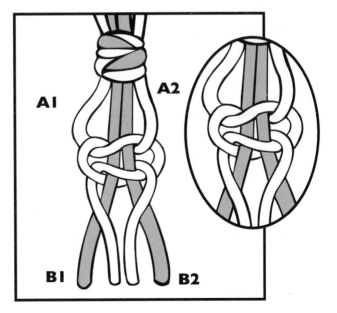

3

ICE CAPS

4 Pick up B1 and bring it over A1 and A2, and then under B2. Pick up B2 and bring it under A1 and A2. Then bring it up through the loop you formed with B1. Pull B1 and B2 up to tighten the knot. You now have a half-knot.

5 Now bring B1 over A1 and A2, and then under B2. Bring B2 under A1 and A2, and then up through the loop you formed with B1.

Pull B1 and B2 up to tighten the knot. Now you have a square-knot. Now move B1 and B2 into the middle. Separate and move A1 and A2 so that they are on the outside.

Keep repeating steps 1-5 until your bracelet is long enough. Tie the 4 strands together, leave a 3-inch (7.6-cm) tail, and trim the rest off.

Tie your *Ice Caps* bracelet around your wrist with a square knot. Now get ready for something *really* hot...

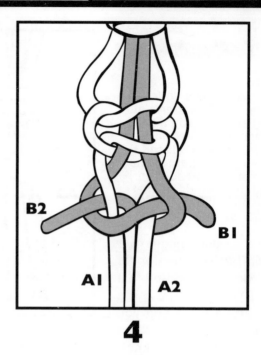

4

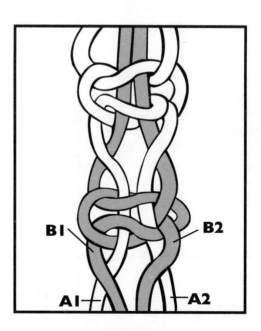

5

SUNCHASER

Even though it's a wide bracelet, making the *Sunchaser* is fun! You'll be using the basic double-knot stitch that you used for the *Tiger Tail.* You'll need two 30-inch (76-cm) strands of 3 colors. Leave a 3-inch (7.6-cm) tail, tie all six strands together, and tape them to a flat surface. Line the strands up in pairs of colors: A1, A2, B1, B2, C1, and C2.

1 Starting from the left with A1, make a row of double knots. See the *Tiger Tail* on page 7 to review how we made the double knots.

Now make a row of double knots with A2. A1 and A2 will then end up on the right.

2 Pick up B1 and make a row of double knots with it. Repeat with B2. B1 and B2 are now on the right.

3 Make a row of double knots with C1, and then C2. You should now have two rows of double knots for each color.

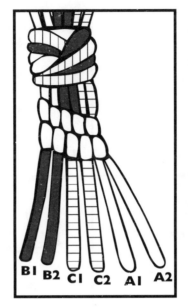

B1 B2 C1 C2 A1 A2

1

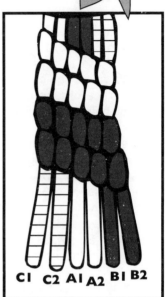

C1 C2 A1 A2 B1 B2

2

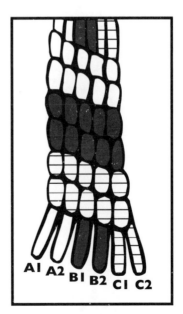

A1 A2 B1 B2 C1 C2

3

4 Leave about ½ inch (1.3 cm) of string without knotting. Flatten the strands out in straight rows. You could put a small piece of tape over this section before continuing.

5 Repeat steps 1-4 until your *Sunchaser* is as long as you like. Tie the 6 strands together, leave a 3-inch (7.6-cm) tail, and trim the rest off.

Tie your *Sunchaser* around your wrist with a square knot.

Are any of your friends cool enough to wear the *Sunchaser*?

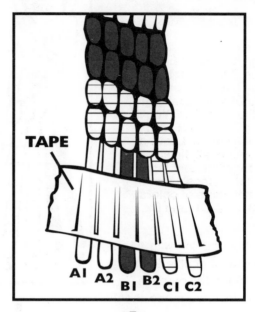

4

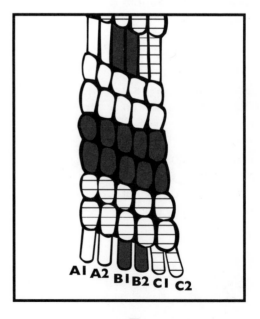

5

HIP CAT

You'll be the hippest cat in town with this cool zigzag bracelet! This pattern uses a basic double-knot stitch.

You'll need two 30-inch (76-cm) strands of 3 colors. Leave a tail and tie all six strands together and tape them to a flat surface.

Line up the strands as follows: A1, B1, B2, A2, C1, and C2

1 Starting from the left with A1, work double knots around B1, B2, A2, C1, and C2. A1 will end up on the far right. Take B1 and work a row of double knots around B2, A2, C1, C2, and A1. B1 will end up on the far right.

2 Continue making rows of double knots with B2, A2, C1 and C2, and so on until you have 6 rows of double knots. The rows will form diagonal lines.

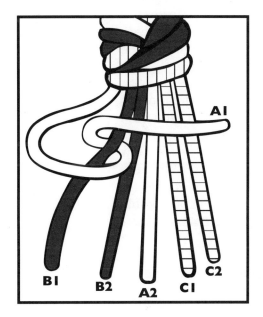

1

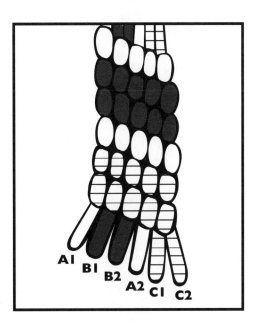

2

HIP CAT

3 When you have 6 rows of double knots, turn the bracelet over so that the back is facing you. Then tape the bracelet down again.

4 Starting on the left again with the same color you last knotted, begin making rows of double knots. The first row after you turn the bracelet over should be pulled tightly. Keep making double knots until you have 6 rows of knots again.

Repeat steps 3-4 until you've turned the bracelet over 6 times. Tie the 6 strands together, leave a 3-inch (7.6-cm) tail, and trim the rest off. Use a square knot to tie your *Hip Cat* around your wrist.

Now try something a little more challenging.

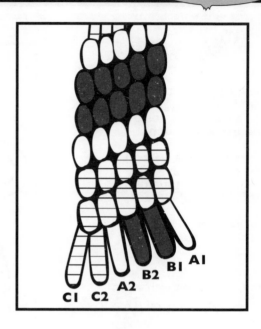

C1 C2 A2 B2 B1 A1

3

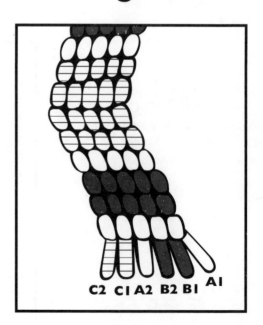

C2 C1 A2 B2 B1 A1

4

SPEED RACER

Making the wild *Speed Racer* is as much fun as a day at the races. Wait until you see how easy it is! You'll need five 30-inch (76-cm) strands of one color, and two 30-inch (76-cm) strands of another color.

Leave a 3-inch (7.6-cm) tail, tie all seven strands together, and tape them to a flat surface. Line the strands up as follows: A1, B1, A2, B2, A3, A4, and A5.

1 Take A4 and make a double knot around A5. Take A3 and make a double knot around A5, and then around A4. Then take B2 and make a double knot around A5, and then around A4.

2 Take A2 and make a double knot around A5, and then around A4. Take B1 and make a double knot around A5, and then around A4. Take A1 and make a double knot around A5, and then around A4.

3 Take A5 and make a double knot around A4. A5 is now on the left and you've made the first half of the "S." Take A5 and make a double knot around A4.

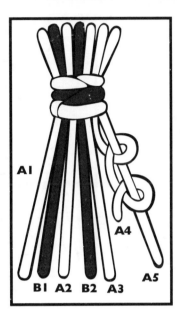

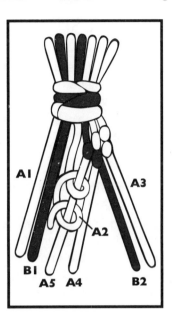

1

2

3

SPEED RACER

4 Take A1 and make a double knot around A4, and then around A5. Take B1 and make a double knot around A4, and then around A5. Take A2 and make a double knot around A4, then around A5.

5 Take B2 and make a double knot around A4, and then around A5. Take A3 and make a double knot around A4, and then around A5. Take A4 and make a double knot around A5. The second half of the "S" is finished!

Keep repeating steps 1-5. Do you see the curves forming?

When your *Speed Racer* is as long as you like, tie the 7 strands together. Leave a 3-inch (7.6-cm) tail, trim the rest off, and use a square knot to tie it closed.

There are even wilder curves ahead when you make the *Surf's Up* bracelet!

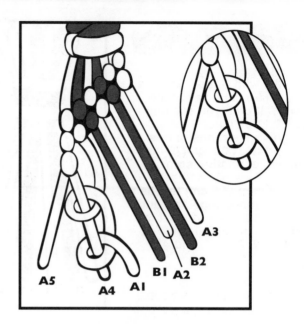

4

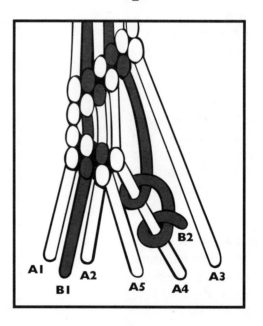

5

SURF'S UP

Hey man, the sun's out and the waves are head high! And if you've already made the *Hip Cat*, then *Surf's Up* will be a breeze! Instead of a six-strand zigzag, *Surf's Up* uses eight strands. The color pattern will also be different because of the way you line the strings up in the beginning.

You'll need two 30-inch (76-cm) strands of 4 colors. Leave a 3-inch (7.6-cm) tail and tie all eight strands together and tape them to a flat surface. Line the strands up in pairs of colors: A1, A2, B1, B2, C1, C2, D1, and D2.

1 Starting from the left with A1, make a row of double knots around A2, B1, B2, C1, C2, D1, and D2. Now make a row of double knots with A2. A1 and A2 will now be on the right.

2 Take B1, and work a row of double knots around B2, C1, C2, D1, D2, A1, and A2. B1 will end up on the far right.

Continue making rows of double knots with B2, C1, C2, D1, D2, until you have 8 rows of double knots. The rows will form diagonal lines.

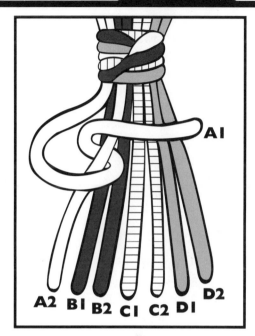

1

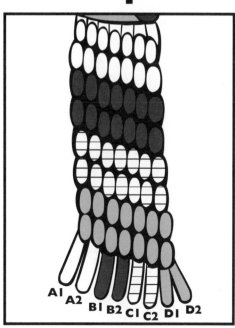

2

SURF'S UP

3 When you have 8 rows of double knots, turn the bracelet over so that the back is facing you. Tape it down again.

Starting on the left again with the same color you last knotted, begin making rows of double knots. Pull the first row tightly after you turn the bracelet over!

4 Keep making double knots until you have 8 rows again. Repeat steps 3 and 4 until you've turned the bracelet over 4 times. Tie the 8 strands together, leave a 3-inch (7.6-cm) tail, and trim the rest off.

Use a square knot to tie this cool bracelet around your wrist.

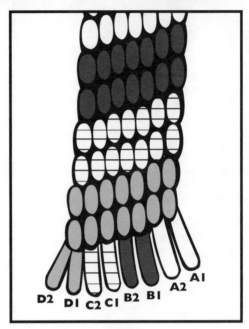

3

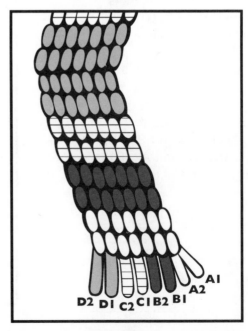

4

ROLLER DERBY

You need seven 30-inch (76-cm) strands. The first 3 strands (A1, A2, and A3) will be three different colors. The second 3 strands (B1, B2, and B3) will be the 3 same colors as the first three.

The last strand (C) should be neutral. Leave a 3-inch (7.6-cm) tail and tie all seven strands together. Tape them to a flat surface. Line the strands up as follows: A1, A2, A3, B1, B2, B3, and C.

1 Take A1 and make one double knot each around A2, A3, B1, B2, B3, and then C. A1 will end up on the right side.

2 Take A2 and make one double knot each around A3, B1, B2, B3, and then C.

3 Take A3 and make one double knot each around B1, B2, B3, and C. Take B1 and make one double knot each around B2, B3, and C. Take B2 and make one double knot each around B3 and C.

4 Take B3 and make a double knot around C and then move it back to the inside. Now the bracelet changes directions. C is on the left.

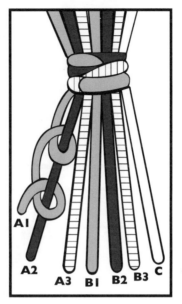

1

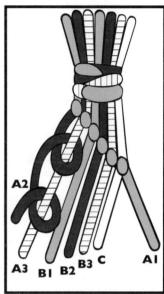

2

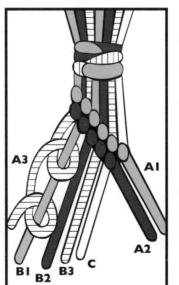

3

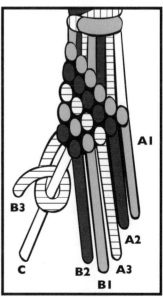

4

ROLLER DERBY

5 Take B3 and make a double knot around C. B3 will now be on the left and C will be on the inside.

6 You just made one half of the "curve."

7 Take B2 and make a double knot around C from the right.

8 Take B1 and make a double knot around C from the right. Keep making rows of double knots around C from the right, using A3, A2, and A1. The first curve is finished! Take B3 and make one double knot each around B2, B1, A3, A2, A1, and C. This will create the first row of the second curve. Keep knotting rows according to steps 2 and 3. When you get to step 4 again with A1, make only a single knot around C. Then make another single knot around C from the right.

9 Finish the second curve by repeating the knots shown in 7 and 8. Repeat steps 1-8, until your *Roller Derby* is as long as you like. Tie the strands together, leave a 3-inch (7.6-cm) tail and trim the rest off. Use a square knot to tie your bracelet closed.

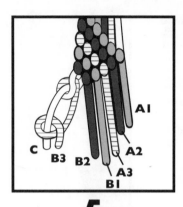

5

6

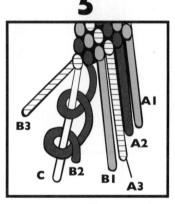

7

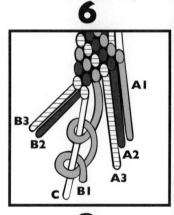

8

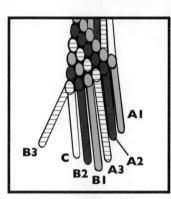

9

BARRACUDA

Take your time – the *Barracuda* is much easier to make than it looks! You'll need two 30-inch (76-cm) strands of 4 colors.

Leave a 3-inch (7.6-cm) tail, tie all eight strands together, and tape them to a flat surface. Line the strands up like this: A1, B1, C1, D1, D2, C2, B2, and A2.

1 Start on the left with A1 and make double knots around B1, C1, and D1. Then go to the right and pick up A2. Double knot A2 around B2, C2, and D2. Finally, with A1, make a double knot around A2. The knots should create an arrow, pointing down.

2 Continue making three more arrows – one with B1 and B2, one with C1 and C2, and one with D1 and D2. The last arrow in color D will be the tail of the *Barracuda*. Then pick up A2 on the left and make a double knot around B2, and another double knot around B2 from the inside.

Now go to the right and with A1, make a double knot around B1. Make another double knot with A1 around B1 from the inside.

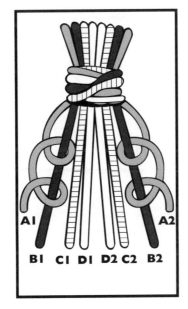

1

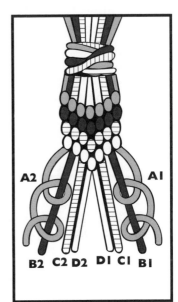

2

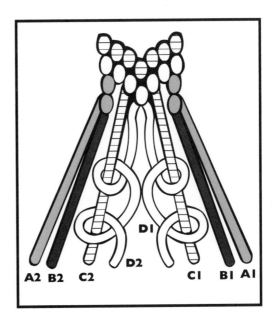

3

BARRACUDA

3 Pick up D2 and make a double knot around C2, B2, and A2. Now pick up D1 and make a double knot around C1, B1, and then A1. This will start the body of the *Barracuda.*

4 Pick up C2 and make a double knot around C1. Then with C1, work double knots from the left around B2 and A2. With C2, make a double knot around B1, and then A1.

5 Pick up B2 and make a double knot around B1. With B1, make a double knot from the left around A2. Pick up B2, and make a double knot around A1.

6 Pick up A2 and make a double knot around A1.

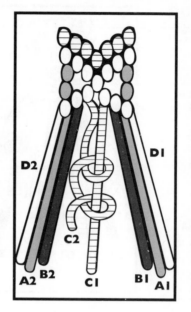

4

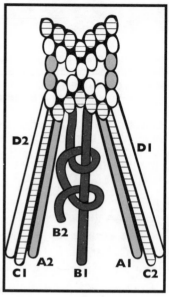

5

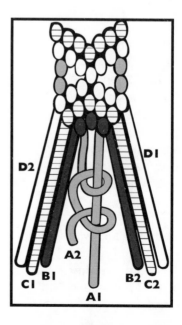

6

7 Pick up B1 and make a double knot around A1. Go to the right side and pick up B2. Make a double knot from the right around A2. Finally, with B1, make a double knot around B2.

8 Pick up C1 and make a double knot around A1, and then B2. Now pick up C2. Make double knots from the right around A2 and then B1. Finally, with C1, make a double knot around C2.

9 Pick up D2 and make double knots around A1, B2, and C2. Now pick up D1. Make double knots from the right around A2, B1, and C1. Finally, with D2, make a double knot around D1. The first *Barracuda* is finished.

0 Repeat steps 1-9 until you have 4 or 5 barracudas. Then finish with 3 arrows (*see steps 1 and 2*). Tie the 8 strands together, leave a 3-inch (7.6-cm) tail, and trim the rest off. Use a square knot to tie this wild *Barracuda* bracelet closed.

Wow – you did a great job!

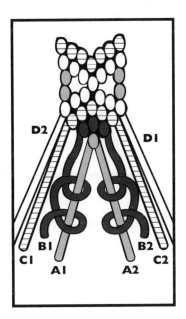

7

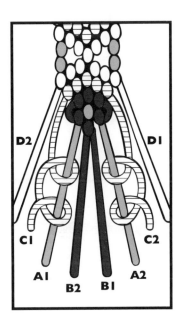

8

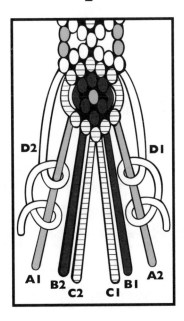

9

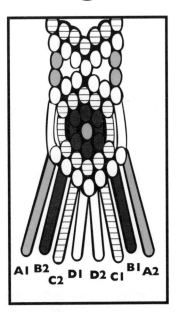

10

All-New Friendship Bracelets

Hot Twist

Tiger Tail

The Popsicle

Ice Caps

Sunchaser

Hip Cat

Speed Racer

Surf's Up

Roller Derby

Barracuda